luca zecchin

the architecture of matisse

(un) searchable depths and minglings

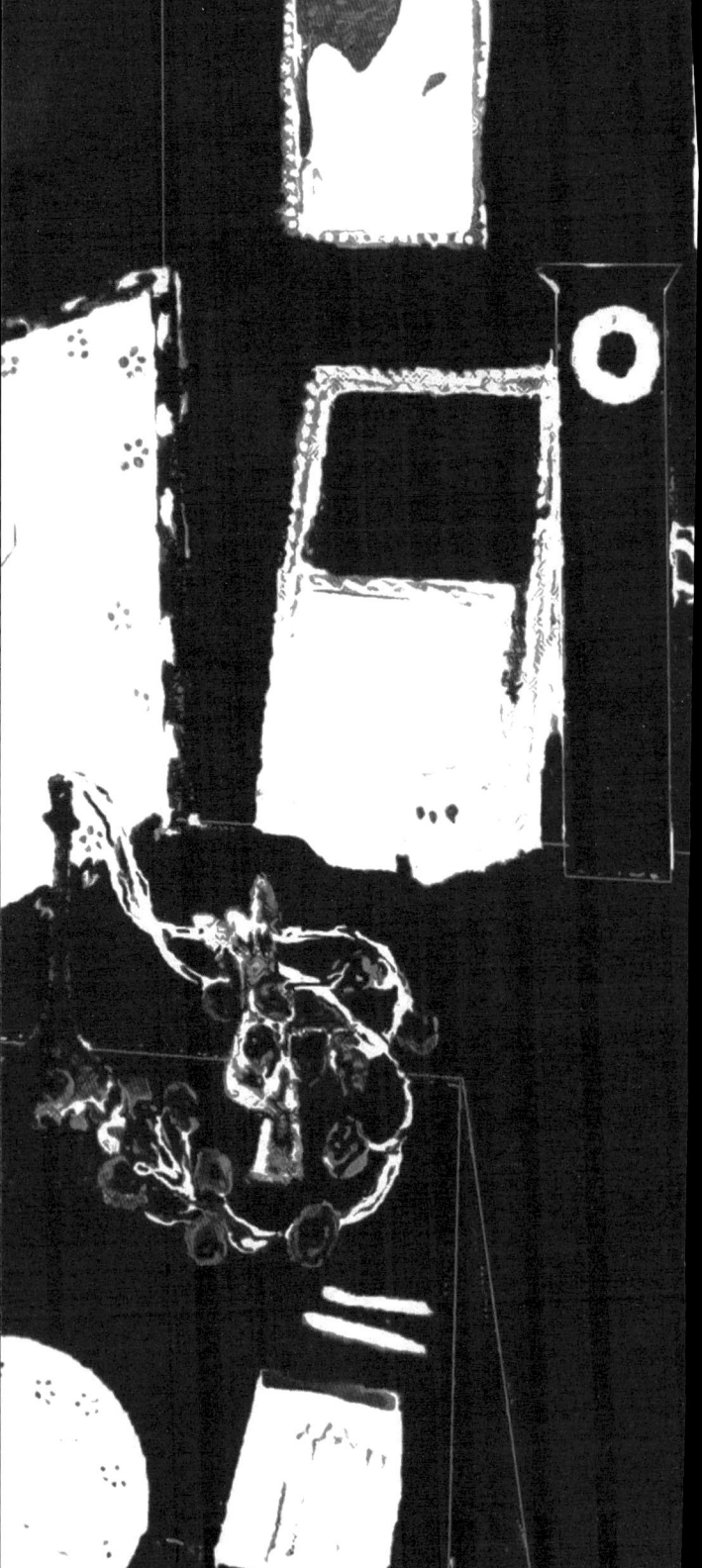

contents

tensions	5
rooms	11
thicknesses	19
relationships	28
combinations	37
minglings	43
fragments	*47*
references	*58*

tensions

The moments of crisis allow us to see. The strength and influence of fragile conditions require to change our gaze on what surrounds us, showing the usefulness of investigating and exploiting its possibilities, researching delicate and hybrid balances. These characteristics seem to outline the paradigm of contemporaneity: a condition of tension that can be translated into spatial conceptions of what is forced to fluctuate to accommodate new instantaneous arrangements, meeting the beauty in what the life transformed.
Within the crisis and ambiguity that characterizes different aspects of our time, this is a reflection on the relationship between the Henri Matisse's pictorial work - grown within the crisis of the twentieth century - and the outline in contemporary architecture of a research characterized by overlaps and incursions, interferences and contaminations that assumes the theme of phenomenology and refined relations between elements, the composition with the objects of reality, the work on the physical and

conceptual margins of things, as essential questions able to condensing spatial values of great interest.

In order to make precious this approach, it is essential to premise a momentary suspension of the essential difference between the processes and the conditions in which we works in architecture compared to those of the painting (Gregotti, 2011). In fact, it is clear that while for the painting the use of expressive tools moves within a two-dimensional plane, an autonomous surface that, as Michel Foucault says, can be freed from the rules of three-dimensionality (Foucault, 1966), for the architecture the instruments are aimed at the organization of a significant space, thanks to techniques and for the life that it welcomes.

However, this reflection starts from the belief that architecture is, at the origin, a *modus operandi* of thought, a way of seeing the things of reality and of weave those relationships that are useful in obtaining reading keys and fertile imaginaries to further thoughts; which are projects and architectures. And the need is to clarify the reasons for an interest in some expressive outcomes that seem to have never touched, rediscovering the reasons of such attraction in the analogies between what I think to be the matissian process of the painting construction and some principles that appear useful to the project of contemporaneity.

This reflection starts from the architectural interior space, from the edge as a habitable place and from the scale as a relational one, but keeping in mind the possibility of cultivating a fruitful ambiguity; because the issue can be extended and the reasoning turned up outside architecture, in the city, the open space, the landscape. We live in a layered interior space saturated of *mark* - space between spaces - where all that has become background, discarded or contrasted, emerges with force. Even the ugly and the fault, the impure and the partial, the bad and the *unpresentable*, the time and the death, the reopening of the work and the unfinished as a possibility of another completion, the life that transforms architecture beyond the architect, they can become the values of a *design resistance*, generators of other ways of being, of new completions.

The second nature in which we live is an interior space, an artifact where we can *only turn inside* (Derrida, 1968), saturated with everything that has remained, often accepted, as a background. And the project is increasingly called to emerge in "the correlation between objects, the specific character of each, modified in relation to others" (Stein, 1908), to experience an *exploration on the contrary*, a "peripheral vision" (Barr, 1951) able to sound out those marginal territories where a tension fits in, with which to re-build "the space and the movement" (Bocchi, 2010).

The subject and the background can return to have the same value (Matisse, Courthin, 1941) and the architecture of this interior can have different shapes and still fulfill their tasks, like for instance a drawer, it can have many different shapes - it has margins depths - and still be a drawer where people live with their things. This is what Matisse suggests in the series of paintings characterized by the presence of a glass ball with *Red fish* (1911). The counterpoint between the frontal and profile view of the fish, describes at the same time the simultaneity of the content and reveals each "possible possible". This issue affects Emilio Cecchi, who entitled *Pesci rossi* (Cecchi, 1920) his collection of short texts and notes with which he questions us. What is more trivial than a glass ball with fish? It is one of the many objects of our life that we look without seeing, saturated of insignificance. But we can reverse the game, question and transform indifference into wonder, to evoke scenarios available to new completions. The red fishes are normal until we look at them in profile, but a sudden look put them in front and everything changes. Fronts appear to us like something else, hidden in the most obvious appearances. This attendant attitude highlights the possibility of to seize a gap, a margin between the things of reality. They always hide a supplement, a presence of imperceptible and potential metamorphosis.The horoscope of this way of seeing - and composing - could be usefully extended to architecture, with the ability to make a place of minglings, of frugal compromises, *durchdringung* (Benjamin, 1963), and thus essentially a relational device.

As Steven Holl argues, it is necessary to "develop the possibility of a collection of things mixed together in a new way, where the horizon is open and merges both with the inside and outside" (Holl, 2000). A relationship that for Matisse must always be achieved with the smallest number of tools, because "no element can be superfluous, because each thing that is added removes meaningfulness to the rest" (Matisse, 1908).

The matissian tools are the tensioned "common places", driven to the essential: lines, colors, relationships (margins, matters, voids). For Matisse, it is necessary to find the "purity" necessary "when the technical tools have so refined to sterilize their power" (Matisse, Courthin, 1941), a non-formalistic "purity", but due to the principles (Matisse, 1907). Because "what matters most are the relationships (...). Music and color follow parallel paths: seven notes, with some modifications, are enough to write any music score: why the same should not happen to the plastic art?" (Matisse, 1947).

Beyond the transpositions, Matisse's research is evidently a continuous recall to create new completions with the specific tools of his discipline. And this in architecture binds the problem of building "poetically" with reality, with the *second nature* that demands quality and care (Heidegger, 1991): of the project that make possible to live and to feel space; of the construction as art that holds together; of the composition as mixing and amalgamation of things and heterogeneous parts.

rooms

For Matisse, Nature as such is no longer represented. He affirms the impossibility of continuing to copy Nature: "I am forced to interpret and submit to the spirit of the painting. When I have found all the relationships between the tones, resulting a living chromatic agreement, a harmony similar to that of a musical composition" (Matisse, 1908). "We have just emerged from the realistic movement that has gathered many materials" (Matisse, 1909).
Matisse's goal is to overcome the collection and propose a new synthesis. "Realists and Impressionists copy from Nature; all their art lies in the truth, in the exactness of the representation.

(...) In Nature I take what I need, then combine all the effects, balancing them in description and color" (Matisse, 1909). The architectural belly becomes the paradigmatic place where he investigates a new condition, the result of the "amalgam" (Matisse, 1909) of objects, spaces and life.

The reality from which he starts, is returned re-signified through the work on relationships between things and the construction of a different space-world, an archipelago of interiors that build another nature with their own laws (Contardi, 2006). From the *Seville still life* (1910) to the *Gouaches découpées* (1946), Matisse shows in the joyful contamination of the space with hybrid, fragile elements, the possibility of reaching a re-founding timeless dimension, hence more real.

The matissian interiors condense a "domestic" character that we can connect to the ability of architecture to make space, to define an empty space. It is the empty space represented by Luigi Moretti (1950) in the architecture described in negative, through cavities. Because even when space is empty, life turns it into a full one. This is the full space meticulously described by Georges Perec in the *Life a User's Manual* (Perec, 1978) and summarizes by Paul Steinberg in the cover image of the novel. The protagonist is the architecture that welcomes the lives of its inhabitants on June 23, 1975, at 8 o'clock, in a Parisian palace of the imaginary rue Simon-Crubelier 11. The architecture is shown in section - 100 rooms, 99 of which is devoted to a chapter - as a narrative and relational device.

The correlation between space, objects and life is what distinguishes the architectural sections painted by Matisse.

According to Lauren Mahony (Mahony, 2015), these paintings clearly show that the cozy interiors, apparently random, are at the same time "the study of a painter and a home space" as in *Dancer resting* (1939-1940).

In *The red studio* (1911), art and decorative objects are painted solidly in color and in detail, while the room's architecture and furnishings are linear diagrams indicated only by negative gaps in the red surface. Time is suspended in this magical space defined by ethereal lines and subtle spatial discontinuities of a private universe. With the lack of perspective Matisse intentionally violates the principles of visual truth to better balance the relationships, empty spaces and hybridization between things are made more evident by the unifying color field that gathers different spatial areas. The wallpaper and the tablecloth are the same tissue, the objects acquire an ambiguous scale, the natural-artificial figures are repeated and cross over the room limits. The window frames an outside traced as a fragment, such as a painting hanging on the wall, a close-up, a photographic zoom.

None of the matissian objects seem particularly luxurious, they are rather *wabi-sabi* things, their value lies in the relationships they establish between them and the possibility of living space. *Wabi-sabi* things (Koren, 2002) are vulnerable, they affect minor and hidden aspects, including temporary and ephemeral, blurred and evanescent. They show the signs of suffer time, wear and imperfections. They are ordinary "full spaces", everyday objects of the lived time.

According to Gaston Bachelard, they are "very simple images, happy space images": small and collected places like those illustrated by the English tales of Beatrix Potter (1956). These spaces ask us to approach, to touch, to get in touch with them, because they are the containers where we place our lives and our things, where values are collected and enriched.

They are the Matisse's beloved spaces, because "we must love space to describe it so thoroughly" (Bachelard, 1957) and to express it. They are containers, drawers, because as every "furniture poet" instinctively knows, an interior is deep, it is "a space of intimacy, a space that does not open in front of anyone" (Bachelard, 1957). Like Man Ray's *Photograms and Radiographs* (1918), they are suitcases that keep things together, those found, those collected.

In Matisse's empty/full spaces everything is collected and condensed, almost crushed to the margins without occupying space, in a protected dimension. Objects are boiling, suggesting margins to welcome them, releasing the space they are simultaneously activated. This architecture is a mantle, "the great comes out the small, not from the logical law of a dialectic of opposites, but by the liberation from every obligation of size, a liberation which is the very characteristic of imagination" (Bachelard, 1957) as in the *Madonna della misericordia* by Piero della Francesca (1460) where the great mantle holds together and takes care of them: a wall that contains.

The architecture of Matisse is a drawer, a microcosm that contains and connects, as in *Large red interior* (1948). And despite the art of Matisse has long been wiped out as pure decoration - his phrase "I dream an art of balance, purity, tranquility (...) a good armchair to rest from physical fatigue" is known such as the damage that this unhappy metaphor caused him - we can reread in his architecture the non-eliminable need to taming the space to be able to live in.

As *San Girolamo nel suo studio* by Antonello da Messina (1474-1475) "the whole space is organized around a furniture (...) the furniture defines a domesticated space where cats, books, and men live serenely" (Perec, 1974), a place that becomes "available for minimal, daily life gestures, but loaded with a profound sense of humanity" (Lejard, 1948). All of these thicknesses are architectures that collect small cosmos and contain the attributes of greatness. The greatness mentioned by Gottfried Semper, not the big thing, but the one that evokes the "sentiment of the refuge" (Hermann, 1990), the container that mixes with the contents. And among the many objects that the architecture of Matisse holds together, those of Nature play an essential role. This role offers itself to a reflection on the relationship between the two terms - nature, artifice - that marks reality and therefore architecture today.

Interior with Egyptian curtain (1948) contains three natures: the first is the one seen through the window, in a similar-zenith vision; the second is that of the fruit on the table; the third is that of the Egyptian curtain that is in-between the two previous ones, a kind of natural artifact.

In Matisse, nature and artifice, in their different combinatorial degrees, are always integrated into a single "constellation" of interacting figures, such as in *Interior with aubergines* (1911) where the mingling results from the different natures that touch each other; to the edge of the frame, removed by the same contamination (Barr, 1974).

The pink studio (1911) shows a further multiplicative synthesis, the proliferation of elements in space deconstructs the hierarchies, suppressing every distinction between the two terms, between architecture and landscape, as in *Red interior still life on a blue table* (1947).

In some cases, nature and artifice are spaced into a vision that framed the measure of a relationship, as in *Interior in venetian red* (1946). In other cases, the bundle becomes a transition, succession of folded spaces as in *Interior with phonograph* (1924) where the different nature of objects and spaces are confused.

As Yve-Alain Bois has well clarified (Bois, 1998), the decorative aspect in Matisse is identified by the expansive force of painting, the size assumed by his paintings beyond the real dimensions. It is a conscious and researched character, which stems from the tension of relationships between different things. "I don't paint things. I only paint the difference between things" (Matisse, 1908) explains Matisse by revising the idea of Degas on the substance of the ornament as an interval and a relation between elements. As in the *Red Room* (1908), reliving this substance into a positive way, the architecture of Matisse declares that it does not aspire to self-sufficiency, but rather experiences a new concept of artifact.

It is an artifact that defeats the environment: where all the elements belong to the same ecology. And the pre-eminence of relationships between things makes us lose sight of the subject, because the true subject is constituted by the relationships themselves, the meant amalgam as the possible organization of a coexistence, of a polite compromised. The compositional center is emptied of weight, the marginal emerges with all the perturbing elements of space.

thicknesses

In the *Dances* (1909-1910) the black margins of the figures are dense contours that, in their mutual agreement with the empty space, stand out while bind. This is the line described by Paul Signac (Contardi, 2006) as "a good finger thick", a seemingly inaccurate and (un) searchable space because, as

Matisse says, "precision is not the truth", but "it is by entering the object that we enter into ourselves" and "the voids can serve as corrections" (Stein, 1908).

In architecture, reasoning on the margin means thinking about the thickness of certain spaces, their disposition, and the ability to interact with other spaces; how a margin is, or can to be generated, altered, used, destroyed. And how it is or can be perceived, identified, redefined. I first start from the meaning of the term: the margin is the extreme, the edge of a qualitatively delimited area, the white space *màrgo* between which is placed the text on the page, the welding or the scar of a wound, the boundary *mark* between spaces. Margins are the primary element of our perception, representation and construction of reality.

As Gregory Batenson argues, "perception operates only upon difference. All the receipt of information is necessarily the receipt of differences, and all the perception of differences is limited by thresholds" (Bateson, 1979). As perception is the distinction of the margins of figures, the construction is primarily the configuration of the space.

Perceiving or configuring a margin refers to the action of marking lines. And in Matisse the line defines and delimits without necessarily closing. In the *Ink drawings* (1941) there is an "essential" continuity (Cherix, Julliard, 2007) between the represented masses and the white on paper.

Similarly, in *Black-out surveys* (1944) - an almost misguided path by Matisse - the inversion between the full and the empty become "light generators" (Matisse, 1939) of a conceptually invisible space. He argues that "one must always pursue the interest of the line where one wants to enter, where he wants to die, what is its source. Never forget the constructive lines! Construction has to be there right away. Each line must have a function (...) lines must play harmony and counterpoint, such as music. The line cannot exist alone, always brings a companion to itself; a line does not express anything, only in relation to another creates volume "(Stein, 1908).

In Matisse paintings the line is always a thickness, the margin of color scores is a generative element always present, not rebuilt with the background from the inside, as in Cézanne. In *Joie de vivre*

(1906), the approach of the dark line that delimits the figures with the transparency of the canvas, makes vibrant the contour and transforms it into a depth with a its own life.

This feature approaches to a precise architectural conception, the one that makes of the edge a living space. These are devices for contermination, "walls" that mark a here and a there.

Even if they belong to the contour, such as the burden of a coarse and thick tissue, they have a significant their own role.

This new architectural place is the result of an evolution that is together a synthesis between three "wall" concepts. The first belongs to the Roman wall: a large and continuous mass that is transformed into the negative space of an inner volume.

The second one belongs to the Renaissance concept where the research focuses on the decomposition of the monolithic wall, restored as a sum of independent plans reconstructed according to the principles of perspective; as Colin Rowe (1993) points out, mesh, structure, texture and grid are brought to a bas-relief, a kind of architectural *stiacciato* where the mass is *exfoliated* in compressed layers, anticipating the idea of deep façade and of a wall as a container of places.

The third corresponds to the modern wall freed from static constraints, where the research is aimed at a succession of intervals between interior and exterior, an interface that accommodates spaces of disjunction between the closing elements and the structural ones.

In contemporary combinatorial synthesis, the mass remains minimal, optimized and in some cases reduced to the essential, but the thickness grows exponentially. It is a clear and obvious thickness, increased to become a living, transitory and usable space.

Analogous considerations can be extended to horizontal, covering and ground planes in which the conception of a complex whole becomes place, an active space.

The conquest of the margin space, such as the matissian edges, refers to the large number of secondary spaces that can be obtained within the thickness of the construction, hidden or open from time to time on the inside or outside.

The thickness of the edge and its ability to contain places are at the basis of several architectural researches designed to express the voids of the project in a positive way.

In some cases it is a question of technical or structural needs, the need to accommodate all the service elements necessary for the operation of a building. As Rem Koolhaas argues in *Last Apples. Speculations on structure and services*, the system of "big walls" is the new material that allows to individualize the architectural interior and "section becomes a battlefield; white and black openly fight for dominance (in some buildings the section black bands exceed 50% of the total). The black zone is not only strictly useless for future occupants of the building, but if it is conceivably inaccessible to the architect who has become an intruder in the project; occult, its dominion is the mere residue of the demands of others" (Koolhaas, 1993).

The architecture of the (un) searcheable depth can make it habitable a thickness otherwise inaccessible or even invisible. The margin is the privileged place for the architect's work; the penetration of empty into the full is the goal of a work that considers a different relationship between full and empty, black and white, visible and invisible, inside and outside.

Man is by definition incomplete and needs of necessary accessories. The margin can be container of smaller objects and places while it separates functions.

The need to open and close a space and to preserve the necessary objects for its operation without occupying it, their conformation as places from which to observe and to stay in a special way, make the architectonic devices of/in the marginal spaces deeply needed and no superfluous, intense and precious: the margin becomes space in the complete possibility of the existence of objects and people.

Through digging, folding, doubling, it can accommodate marginal bellies that equip a domesticated space, "domestic" stratagems to order space without occupying it. It is the poetics of a non-correspondence between figures, in which the matter thickens at the edges, as in a Matisse room. The increase in thickness to contain other small rooms makes the margin a space that is always understood as "in-between", a dialectic relationship between content and container in which the spacing and excavation operations have saved only a few masses of the original volume, by modulating a phenomenological place made of matter and light. The possibility of a progressive enlargement to increase its space capacity, the use of sufficiently large spaces to be crossed and to live in, the reading in depth applied to the different scales of the project, can be stretched beyond the limits of the construction and landing in the open space, the city, the landscape. Luis Kahn, for example, speaks about marginal spaces that covering the architecture with empty spaces "in ruins" and that must be seen only through.

The construction of two distinct profiles, internal-internal and outside-outside, generates transition places, "spaces (...) without a particular use, so much so than one can talk of marginal or resulting voids, compared by Kahn himself to the character both ambiguous and deprived of specific functional connotations of antique ruins" (Kahn, 2003), because what has become a ruin is again free of the bond of function.

They are architectures where the margin

is modeled through the dialectics between the two geometries of the container and content, realizing the possibility to live the space between wall, no longer residual but as a life resource.

Using these concepts, habitable spaces are conceived in places that are usually considered uninhabitable: walk-in spaces, wall-diaphragm, enclosures to be crossed without specific connotations of use. In other cases the circulation and the architecture of the margin becomes a sequence of folded spaces, enlarged, duplicated, complicated within a conceptually infinite thickness.

As a *Sponge of Menger*, they are spongy structures, *volumetric balls* woven by voids with different thickness, spaces folded on themselves that envelop limbs and interiors in a continuous contact. And as Gilles Deleuze writes, "the hole is the place of the thinner matter" - like the canvas deliberately left untouched by Matisse between the black line and the color *a l'à plat* - margin architectures conform by differences of density, of perceptual phenomenologies, of sensitive relationships.

relationships

Pragmatically, the margin is needed to expand, clarify, and shade the main body of a space, like a text.

The margin is a liminal presence from which an internal belly is demarcated, contrasted or aligned with another interior. In a broader sense, it represents a critical distance, a range that allows a fruition.

This identity-oxymoron allows us to recognize it as the place of touch (Merleau-Ponty, 1964) where opposites co-exist. Because touch without being touched is impossible.

The architect Alberto Perez-Gomes describes the *chora* as a unique sort of space: a container where things take shape, like the maternal abdomen during motherhood, that is shapeless in itself because it does not have a permanent identity (Pérez-Gómez, Parcell, 1997).

Also Jacques Derrida interprets the *chora* as the space that produces differences, an interval that allows things to have a place where they can happen. "*Chora* receives everything or gives

place to everything, yet Plato insists that in fact it has to be a virgin place, and that it has to be totally foreign, totally exterior to anything that it receives; so, in a sense, it does not receive anything
- it does not receive what it receives nor does it give what it gives." (Derrida, 1993).
Margins are fundamental as relationship places, because a margin is above all a place where can be play movement and change; a place where physical and visual alternations are stronger and can take advantage of the neighboring places.
The theme is a critical question that emerges in architectures and landscapes where matter thickens to the edges, leaving the marginal void available. The margin have body, complexity and meaning in itself, and does not diminish to the mere separation of two realities. It is a spatial entity within which one recognizes and explores, at the same time, the possibility of living on a different scale.
The scale problem is therefore central. Reasoning in scale does not mean only reasoning in terms of magnitude or

size. The magnitude is the largest or the smallest dimensional volume of a thing, an objective dimension, with a quantifiable and real measure in terms of height and depth.

On a map or a drawing, the scale is the straight line divided into equal parts representing meters or kilometers; it serves to measure proportionally the real measures of what is represented. The scale is the size of a drawing according to metric or proportion in which a plan is developed; it is the relationship between topographic representation and real distances.

The scale is a relation between certain quantities and units. Each object of reality has consistent and precise measures, but its scale depends on the choice of a system of optimal proportions, traditionally recognized in the "principle of similarity" that governs the relationship between growth and form in Nature.

In architecture, the scale is the aspect that makes it intelligible by giving us an idea of how to relate to it. And it does it by reinforcing or contradicting our perception. For Matisse the composition has to change according to the surface to be filled, "in *Dance for Bernes* I made the characters bigger than the real (...) because I used fragments" (Matisse, 1947), "I would not repeat the same drawing on a sheet of different sizes" because "the various signs must be balanced so that they do not destroy each other" (Matisse, 1908).

In this regard Maurice Merleau-Ponty writes of a film that recorded the work of Matisse as the artist was drawing. The film is entitled *Matisse or A visit with Matisse* (1946) and is a documentary study of the artist made in Paris and Vence.

The most striking sequences, partly in slow motion, show Matisse drawing a flower that he has just picked in his garden. Here is what Matisse himself told to the journalist and art historian Rosamond Bernier in 1949. "There was a passage showing me drawing in slow motion. Before my pencil ever touched the paper, my hand made a strange journey of its own. I never realized before thah I did this. I suddenly felt as if I were shown naked - that everyone could see this - it made me deeply ashamed. You must understand this was no hesitation. I was unconsciously establishing the relationship between the subject I was about to draw and the size of my paper" (Bois, 1993).

The scale is a relationship that considers contingent and expressive reasons, a relationship between an object - architecture is one of them - and the size of the human body.

When in architecturen, we speak about the scale, we refer to a system that connects the parts and we with them.

In the lessons at the Academy of Paris, Matisse explains that "everything must be constructed with parts that form a whole, and in our work we must include technical knowledge, contemplation of the model or other subject, and the imagination that enriches them. (...) Pay attention to the proportions, but do not sacrifice the sentiment to the correctness. Understanding the essential characteristics (...) the mechanism of construction consists in establishing the oppositions that create the balance between the directions" (Stein, 1908).

If in the physical world is the gravity that controls the form of all organisms, by modifying the morphology as the mass varies, in the articulation of a space, the scalar control can correspond to the laws of perception and movement; read about the interaction of man with the environment, the visual satisfaction of the observer, his sensitive participation in the architectural work.

Today, in architecture, the meaning of scale is changed, amplify. This makes thinkable spaces where there is no scale, the scale is many, or where it is ambiguous.

The new project materials, also the *advanced* coming from other disciplines, produce spaces that do not have a precise reference to existing ones. The classical harmonic relationship between the parts is canceled, the concept of scale is forced. An architectural piece can, for example, appear without scale or with an ambiguous scale when the facade does not reveal what is happening inside, when it is conceived as a monomateric piece, enlarging or reducing other pieces of Nature. Until the research on materialization and transmutation of the architectural body into an interactive and changing relationship between architecture and environment. Here, architecture is a device that produces phenomena, landscapes, which makes visible the flow of time and environmental factors, an architecture that becomes seasonal, mutant material that is dying and reborn.

As *Alice in Wonderland* by Lewis Carrol (1920), when the space of maximum spatial contrast is reached, one enters in a microcosm where everything can be different, even the reference scale. In this type of multi-dimensional, phenomenological space, unity and multiplicity merge into an infinitely porous, spongy or cavernous weaving similar to a cave in the cave where every space contains a world.

These are fractal spaces, their size are met in a place between the lines and the plane, between the surfaces and the volumes. They are denser than surfaces, but without getting mussed into a volume. Like an architecture of Matisse, they are spaces formed by several surfaces tending to infinite, but with a total volume tending to zero. The suggestion can be declined as a compositional operation aimed at the spatial promiscuity and at the creation of nothing between the parts, "nothing-in-between", which is not merely the absence of matter, but concerns the *open form-open work* that can establish a different relationship with the time and the non-finished; subsequent subtractions from the total of similar parts.

The product of this operation is a multiplication of significant voids, sponges obtained within thicknesses. And if the difference between the detail and the whole is canceled, there is no reference to a dimension, everything goes to a series in which it is impossible to find out what the origin is; because the detail and the whole have the same value.

It is a self-similitude that can be extended to the relationship between architecture, city, landscape. A relationship that does not use the scale, that is: where the elements and pieces that we recognize, find their relationships in other tools and relationships, for example with geographic facts, ecological issues or climatic events.

As Dominique Perrault argues, the notion of disposition denies the subordination of the elements and implies that there is no scale. Buildings can be small or large. The contextual impositions, the set of information, will define their size (Perrault, 2016). The disappearance of the scale joins a layered material; it is a kind of new *groundscapes* in which ruins overlap over time, a palimpsest of partial cancellations and partial rewritings that find new relationships in the mutual contacts, by building the space around it.

The matissian conception of building the space around it, in contrast to both Picasso's analytical solidity and the abstract structure of Cezanne, leads us to conceive the scale of the project as a result of a combination of layers that are not articulated in an already finished sequence, but stratify in a pre-existing space.

It is the scale of a relational space which pushes the maximum of the chance to experience it, a space that contains objects and life, architectures and landscapes, natures and artifacts, physical and climatic materials; an intensely ecological space that produces phenomena. Because, according to what Steven Holl writes about the *Chapel of Vence* (1949-1951) the only architecture physically constructed by the painter, "Matisse as an architect realized an ineffable space of astonishing intensity" and shows that "the power of Architecture does not depend on bigness, it depends on intensity" (Holl, 2013).

combinations

Matisse identifies in the combinatorial space between nature and artifice the exclusive place of his research. The artifice unfolds and opens up a renewed dialogue of closer contamination with the materials of Nature, to express a "dream always inspired by reality" (Matisse, 1909) that teaches to see. A research that leads to think more creatively about the relationship between nature and artifice. Moving away from the true Nature of Impressionism, Matisse probe with pure tools - the synthetic design, the color matter, the horoscope of relationships - another truth, a combinatorial path that no longer belongs either to one or the other, but that is generated by their experienced and renewed relationship. On the one hand, the urgency to respond to emerging issues related environmental, climatic and ecological crisis, requires action in dimensionally and conceptually radical terms. On the other hand, the reality with which architecture today operates, at least for a large part of the territories we inhabit, is a compromised amalgam where nature can play a projectual and procedural role, starting from reality to return it with a new meaning, in a construction that is just analogous to Nature itself (Matisse, Courthin, 1941). And the *picturesque*, present in many Matisse's pictorial works, suggests a hybrid spatiality, an intense dialogue between architecture, landscape, environment. The project becomes a process of assembling and concatenating sequences that change over time, working with empty spaces, margins, fragments. Existing elements, first selected as in an *abbecedary* (Koolhaas, AMO 2014), can be combined into narrative structures with new elements, thanks to *fragmentation* tools.

After the disease that strikes him in 1941, Matisse lived a "second life" (Alastair, 2014) during which the physical constraints led him to experiment with other tools. This new research is taken up by the theme of *collage*. In the series *Blue nudes* (1952), for example, pieces of ordinary figures are cut out and recomposed directly into the color space according to a *jazz* rhythmic composition. By painting "with scissors", Matisse activates a spontaneity similar to that of music. The figures dance and enter rhythmically into each other, maintaining a delicate balance. As particles suspended in a liquid, they underline an unprecedented cognition of space, amplifying the contrast between the effect of composition and the poverty of the employed tools. Drawing with scissors, "sculpting in the color reminds me the sculptor's work" (Matisse, 1946), "drawing with scissors on previously colored paper sheets, with only one gesture I can associate the line with the color, the contour to the surface" (Verdet, 2011).

Following the instructions of Matisse, Lydia Delectorskaya brush with uniformly vibrant colors, some white sheets of paper and then Matisse, sitting in bed, cut those saturated sheets. After the scissors have released the figures, he put them in a composition with the help of pins on a large sheet of paper. This is how, for example, the *papiers decoupes* of *Jazz* (1943), a book with twenty color charts, are made. Through selection and reassembly operations, Matisse reaches a layered construction of the sense in which the pieces are transformed into a different relational system (MerleauPonty, 1964). The *collage* is *bricolage*, it brings up the unpredictable and the beauty is built like a game: because every game has precise rules. In the *Dance of Barnes* (1930-1932), starting with a reinterpretation of Giotto's frescoes in Padua, Matisse makes for each figure a full-size silhouette and, moving shapes as "pawns in the dama play", tries to "find an order fully satisfactory" (Matisse, 1947). For two years, Matisse places the shapes on a glossy sheet, punctuating and adapting them to the best possible composition, coming to define an "executive project" (Matisse, 1950). The final work is the mechanic translation of a process, almost industrial, translated in a programmatic manner.

The long time of Matisse's elaboration is a common element in architectural design practices, the necessary modifications and rewritings (Alexander, 2002) as in *Still Life with La Danse* (1909). To repeat, in the interval of a temporal difference, means deepening, going deeper, making choices compared to the possibilities that become present, as in the serial reworks of the '30s and '40s.

Some of these series are accompanied by photographic evidence, showing the complexity of the process, the reprocessing work, phase after phase, as for *The Romanian Blouse* or *The Dream* (1940), the result of paper-cutting techniques for compositional combiner purposes.

This work tool and, more generally, the research on a relational project, in architecture refers to the urgency of working on the relationship between existing parts, bodies and natures. Combining together, finding significant links through subtractions, dissonances, juxtapositions and overlays imply a project that covers and discovers the fragments of reality, inserted with their original story and features into a structure that reconfigures them. It is always about establishing a link with the past, the many pasts that accumulates, discovering, maintaining and revitalizing the various forms of deposited time in the spaces, revealing the overlap of old and new layers (VVAA, 2016). It is also about experimenting with the contamination of the techniques and materials of things that become another, consistent with the life that moves around. The recent changes that affect cities and territories, lay at the center of the project the topics of the cure. And the project is the transformation of already existing partial elements, re-cycling and reusing structures with greater creativity and awareness, with more fragile manipulation practices (Battaino, 2011) and marginal tools (Lacaton, Vassal, 2012). The result of which is a more complete and stratified reality, the continuation of the present through a contemporary look, where that margin from which we started in this reflection should be questioned above all through projects that make it visible.

Objects and spaces can be chosen and re-signified by accepting them, digging for layers, textures, figures (Bianchi, Véronique, 2010). In colliding territories (Rowe, 1978) it is necessary to accept the reality of the situation (Smithson, 1970) with all the contradictions and confusions, to do something with them. This is a project that seeks a form of link, a bond, stratified beyond the simple substitution, a cohabitation that relates the object to the environment, artifices and natures. And the contradiction and disorder of heterogeneous fragments inherited from the recent past can be re-linked in *constellations*, as a potential wealth. In the constellation of small and large elements, in fact, the continuity of the whole is still readable through the fragment, an incomplete and open element that finds its balance only in relation to others by intervals, distances: where the figurative quality is based on the relationships rather than on individual objects.

In the *Memory of Oceania* series (1946) the sinuous shapes sway, evoking leaves, floating plants, sponges, algae and corals inspired by a photograph book of Tahiti; "we can not live in a tidy house", Matisse told his friend Tériade in 1929, "we have to go out, into the jungle, to find easier ways to do".

minglings

From the many suggestions presented in Matisse's work we can also learn about a lesson for the architecture today and the need to work with the heterogeneity of our reality, finding new quality minglings, compromises with its figures and imperfections, giving up abstractions to themselves no (more) sustainable, but to create a new beauty from which to generate and derive motivations for new significant completions. The matissian figuration reveals a margin, a gap that lets transpires the sedimentation of life, a mingling that involves first and foremost a transformation of our gaze and a transmutation of the materials of reality: choosing and arranging them, interacting with new ones, combining them into an amalgam, seems to be an essential practice.

Matisse opposes to the analytical research of Cubism, the phenomenology of perception, the participation in the work, the inductive poetics characterized by continuity and discontinuity. The color disposed in wide areas *a l'à plat* such as the *papiers decoupes* and the *collages* construct *architectural structures* that translate an experiential dimension of reality, a differently plausible depth, an ineffable space.

In his works we find clutches and hybrid processes that use the deconstruction of a thought - the continuous line of a patient pictorial work - as a tool to explore it. He is himself to points out that "my work constitutes a whole, my subsequent discoveries complement each other. I use different techniques (...) but the background is the same, each one helps the other" (Lejard, 1948). And this background consists of a deepening project of intervals between things, because " the environment is what creates the object", where the architecture of relationships is more important than the things themselves. Matisse emphasizes that "the object is not too interesting in itself and for itself", rather "the subject is an actor: it can support different roles in ten different paintings. It is not perceived by itself, it evokes a set of elements" (Lejard, 1948), an amalgam where everything is necessary.

The composition with the elements of reality, the work with the physical and conceptual margins of objects and spaces, the project of relationship as an instrument and indispensable end, are the essential acts which, in my opinion, Matisse's research continues to teach us. The matissian imaginary brings us to see what breaks into reality and exploits it as a creative opportunity. The centrality of the phenomenological and relational issue, the importance of a process of experience, the relevance of sensitive knowledge of things, the research in a way of experiencing heterogeneity, the *nature of things* without the *a priori* rationalization, even the sense of imprecision and apparently random, they give us a logical and operational thickness that is particularly fertile to the project. It is a trace that can indicate a path to experienced within the issues and with the tools of architecture today.

* The fragments of paintings, works of art and projects are a re-processing of their reproductions taken from the publications cited in the bibliography whose copyright is to the relative Authors, Museums or Foundations to which the works belong.

fragments*

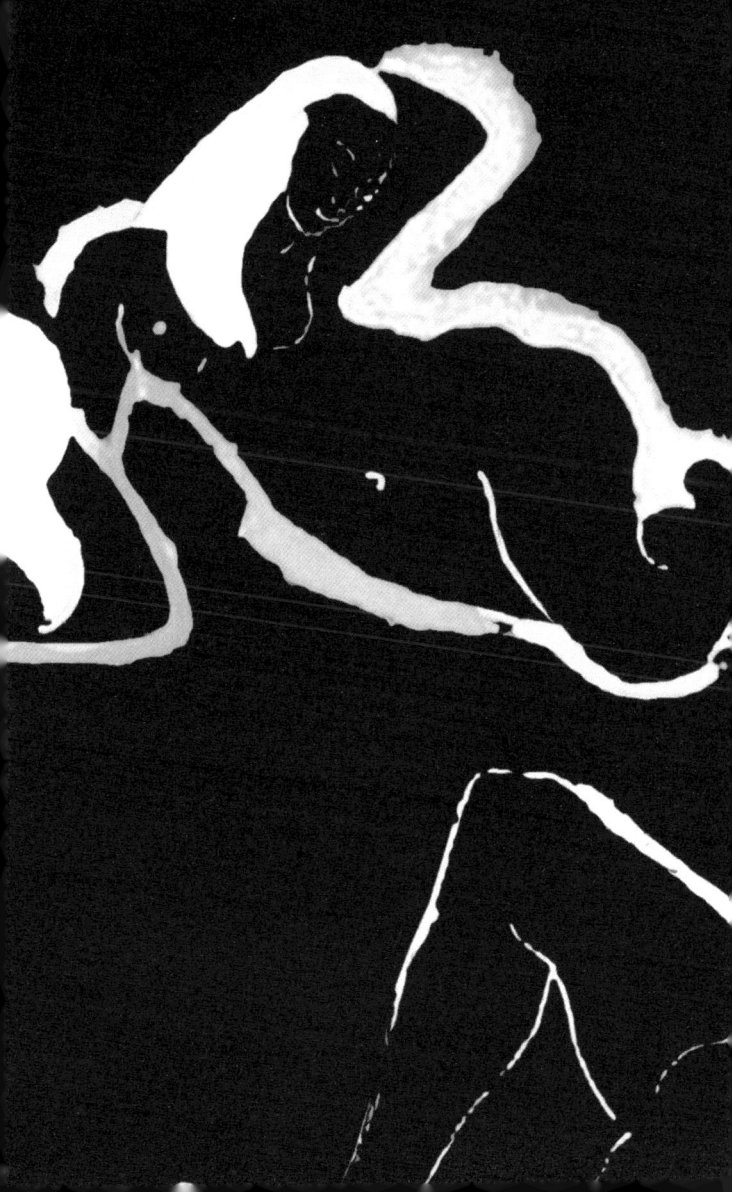

(from left to right, from top to bottom) Fragments of:
1. H. Matisse, *Red fish* (1911); 2. R. Koolhaas, *Conceptual sketch* (1989); 3. H. Matisse, *Seville still life* (1910); 4. H. Matisse, *Gouaches découpées* (1946); 5. L. Moretti, *Model of the empty space of the Basilica of St. Peter in Rome*, (1950); 6. P. Steinberg, *Cover illustration of the novel* Life a User's Manual *by G. Perec* (1978).

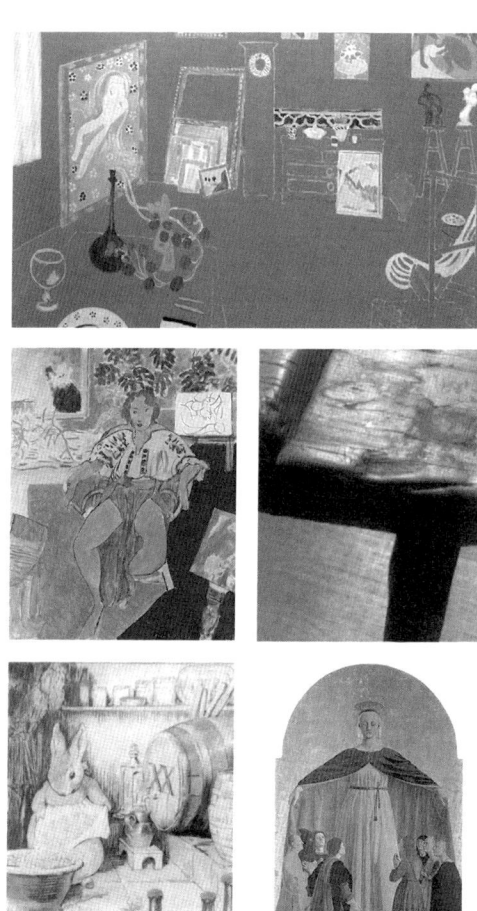

7. H.Matisse, *The red studio* (1911); 8. H. Matisse, *Dancer resting* (1939-1940); 9. L. Koren, *A sofa of wood recovered, with the surface consumed by the use*, from Jurgen Lehi Co Tokyo (2002); 10. P. and A. Smithson, *Reproduction of an illustration of the B. Potter's Stories, From the house of the future to a house for today* (1956); 11. P. della Francesca, *Madonna della misericordia* (1460).

12. H. Matisse, *Large red interior* (1948); 13. A. da Messina, *San Girolamo nel suo studio* (1474-1475); 14. H. Matisse, *Interior with Egyptian curtain* (1948); 15. H. Matisse, *Interior with aubergines* (1911); 16. H. Matisse, *The Pink Studio* (1911); 17. H. Matisse, *Red Interior still life on a blue table* (1947).

18. H. Matisse, *Interior in venetian red* (1946); 19. H. Matisse, *Interior com phonograph* (1924); 20. H. Matisse, *Red room* (1908); 21. H. Matisse, *Ink drawing* (1941); 22. H. Matisse, *Black-out survey* (1944).

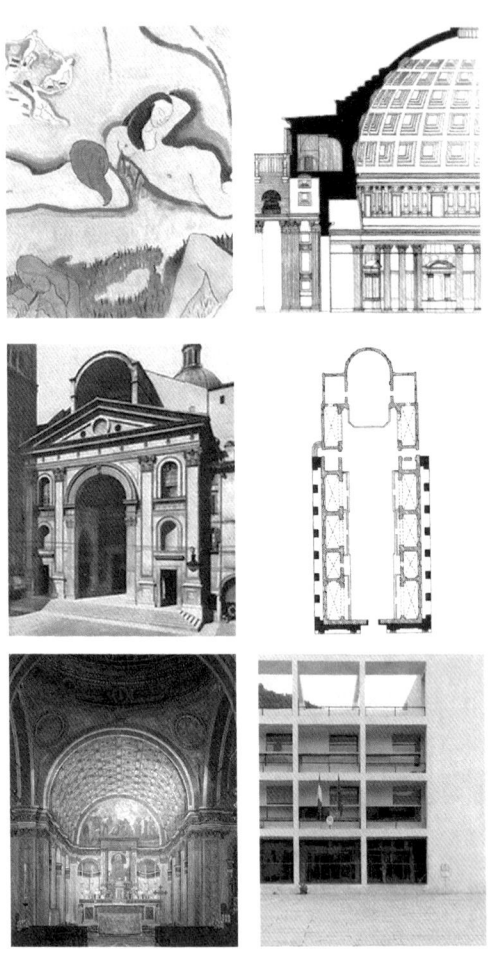

23. H. Matisse, *Joie de vivre* (1906); 24. *Pantheon in Rome* (118-125 d.C.); 25. L.B. Alberti, *St. Andrea in Mantova* (1472); 26. L.B. Alberti, *Tempio malatestiano in Rimini* (1450-1468); 27. D. Bramante, *St. Satiro in Milano* (1482-1486); 28. G. Terragni, *Casa del fascio in Como* (1936).

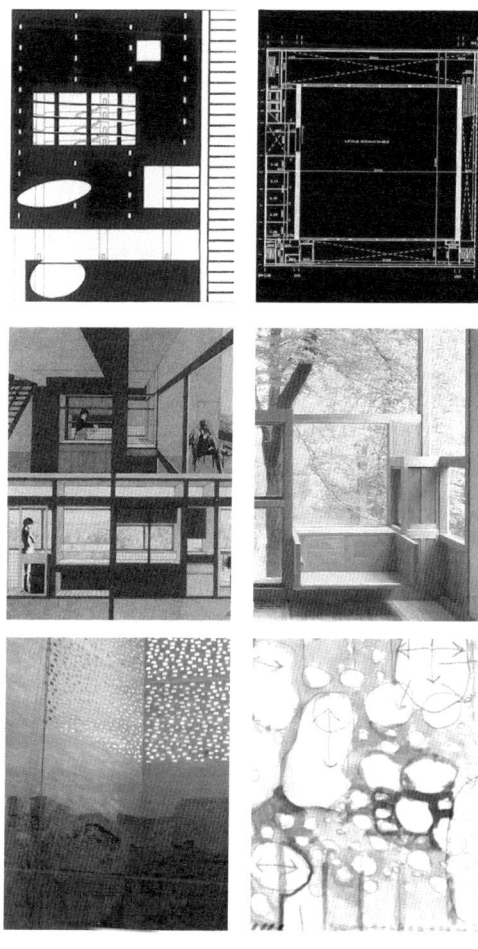

29. R. Koolhaas, *Très Grande Bibliothèque in Paris* (1989); 30. R. Koolhaas, *ZKM center* (1989); 31. Y. Lion and F. Leclercq, *Domus Demain* (1987); 32. L. Kahn, *Fischer house in Philadelphia* (1960); 33. P. Zumthor, *Kolumba museum in Colonia* (2007); 34. S. Holl, *Sketch of a porous space* (2002).

35. A. Mateus, *House in Monsaraz* (2011); 36. MVRDV, *Galaxia IBM* (2001); 37. R. Nishizawa, *House A in Tokyo* (2010). 38. J. Ishigami, *Venice Biennal of Architecture* (2012); 39. H. Matisse, *Dance for Bernes* (1932).

40. R. Koolhaas, *Prada foundations in Milano* (2015); 41. Herzog & De Meuron, *Ricola factory in Mulhouse* (1993); 42. F. J. Kiesler, *David* (1965-1966); 43. K. Schwitters, *Merzbau* (1920-1936); 44. B. Tschumi, *Le Fresnoy* (1991-1997); 45. H. Matisse, *Chepelle du Rosaire in Vence* (1949-1951).

46. H. Matisse, *Blue nudes* (1952); 47. H. Matisse, *Jazz* (1943); 48. H. Matisse, *Still Life with La Danse* (1909); 49. H. Matisse, *The Dream* (1940); 50, H. Matisse, *Memory of Oceania* (1946).

references *(bibliography and iconography)*

Alastair, Sooke 2014. *Henri Matisse. Una seconda vita.* Milano: Electa.
Alexander, Cristofer 2002. *The Nature of Order, vol. I.* Oxford: Center for Environmental Structure Oxford University Press.
Bachelard, Gaston (1957) 1999. *Poetica dello spazio.* Bari: Dedalo.
Barr, Alfred Hamilton (1951) 1974. *Matisse. His art and his public.* New York: Museum of Modern Art.
Bateson, Gregory (1979) 1984. *Mente e Natura. Un'unità necessaria.* It. Ed. Milano: Adelphi.
Battaino, Claudia 2011. *On the margins of permanence. Fragile and relational exercises.* In: Czasopismo Techniczne Architektura, v. 108, n. 15, p. 55-64.
Benjamin, Walter (1963) 2007. *Städtebilder, Suhrkamp Verlag, Frankfurt am Main.* It Ed. *Immagini di città.* Torino: Einaudi.
Bianchi, Matteo, Mauron, Véronique 2010. *Collage. Una poetica del frammento.* Ticino: Pagine d'Arte.
Bocchi, Renato 2010. *Progettare lo spazio e il movimento. Scritti scelti di arte, architettura e paesaggio.* Roma: Gangemi Editore.
Bois, Yve-Alain (1998) 2001. *Matisse and Picasso.* Paris: Ediotis Flammarion.
Bois, Yve-Alain 1993. *Painting as Model.* Cambridge: MIT Press.
Cecchi, Emilio (1920) 2015. *Pesci rossi.* Roma: Elliot Edizioni.
Cherix, Christophe, Julliard, Mayte 2007. *Henri Matisse: Traits essentiels. Monotypes 1906-1952.* Colonia: Walther Koning.
Contardi, Bruno 2006. *Le Danze di Matisse.* Milano: Electa.
Derrida, Jacques (1968) 2007. *La farmacia di Paltone.* It. Ed. Milano: Jaka Book
Derrida, Jacques (1993) 1997. *Il segreto del nome.* It. Ed. Milano: Jaca Book.
Foucault, Michel (1966) 2016. *Le parole e le cose.* It. Ed. Milano: Rizzoli.
Gregotti, Vittorio 2011. *L'architettura di Cézanne.* Milano: Skira.
Heidegger, Martin 1991. *Costruire, abitare, pensare.* On: Vattimo, Gianni edited by. *Martin Heidegger. Saggi e discorsi.* Milano: Ugo Mursia Editore.
Hermann, Wolfgang 1990. *Gottfried Semper. Architettura e teoria.* Milano: Electa.
Holl, Steven (2000) 2004. *Parallax: architettura e percezione.* It. Ed. Milano: Postmedia Books.
Holl, Steven 2013. *Matisse in New York: ineffable space.* On: *32BNY.*

Lacaton, Anne, Vassal, Jean-Philippe, 2012. *Surplus. Conversation with Wellner, Mathieu*. German Pavillon, Biennale Architettura 2012.
Lejard, André 1948. *Henri Matisse*. Paris: Hazan Editions.
Mahony, Lauren 2015. On: Elderfield, John, Galassi, Peter 2015. *In the Studio*. New York: Phaidon Press.
Matisse, Henri 1907. *Intervista di Guillaume Apollinaire*. On: *La Phalange 2*, December 15-18, 1907. Paris.
Matisse, Henri 1908 . *Notes of a Painter*. On: *La Grande Reveu*, 25 December 1908. Introduction by Desvallières, Georges. Eng. Ed. On: Benjamin Roger 1987. *Matisse's Notes of a Painter: criticism, theory and context, 1891-1909*. Umi Research Press.
Matisse, Henri 1909. *Conversazione con Estienne*. On: Matisse, Henri 2014. *Scritti e pensieri sull'arte*. It. Ed. Milano: La Feltrinelli Abscondita.
Matisse, Henri 1939. *Note di un pittore sul suo disegno*. In: *Le Point n. 21*, July 1939.
Matisse, Henri, Courthin, Pierre (1941) 2015. *Henri Matisse: l'intervista perduta*. Milano: Skira.
Matisse, Henri 1947. *Lettere 1940-1947*. On: Matisse, Henri 2014 . Op. cit.
Matisse, Henri 1950. *Entretien avec Georges Charbonnier*. On: Matisse, Henri 2014 . Op. cit.
Merleau-Ponty, Maurice (1964) 1993. *Il visibile e l'invisibile*. It. Ed. Milano: Bompiani, Milano.
Perec, Georges (1974) 2008. *Specie di spazi*. It. Ed. Torino: Bollati Boringhieri.
Perec, Georges (1978) 2005. *La vita istruzioni per l'uso*. It. Ed. Milano: Rizzoli.
Pérez-Gómez, Alberto, Parcell, Stephen 1997. *Chora. Intervals in the Philosophy of Architecture vol.1*. Montréal: McGill-Queen's University Press.
Perrault, Dominique 2016. *Groundscapes: other topographies*. Orléans: Hyx Editions.
Kahn, Louis 2003. *Louis Kahn: essential texts*. Twombly, Robert edited by. New York: W.W. Norton & Company.
Koolhaas, Rem 1993. *Last Apples. Speculations on structure and services*. On: *SMLXL*. Rotterdam: Monacelli Pr.
Koolhaas, Rem, AMO 2014. *Fundamentals*. Venezia: Marsilio.
Koren, Leonard 2002. *Wabi-Sabi per artisti, designer, poeti e filosofi*. Milano: Ponte delle grazie.
Rowe, Colin 1978. *Collage City*. Cambridge: MIT Press.
Smithson, Alison & Peter 1970. *Ordinariness & Light*. Cambridge: MIT Press.
Stein, Sarah 1908. *Appunti tratti dalle lezioni di Matisse*. In: Matisse, Henri 2014 . Op. cit
Verdet, André 2011. *Prestiges de Matisse*. Ticino: Pagine d'Arte
VVAA, 2016. *Unfinished*. Spanish Pavillion. Biennale Architettura 2016. Barcelona: Fundacioà Arquia.

The Architecture of Matisse
(un) Searchable Depths and Minglings

Author
Luca Zecchin

Published by
LISt Lab
info@listlab.eu
listlab.eu

Editorial Director
Alessandro Franceschini

Art Director & Production
Blacklist Creative, BCN
blacklist-creative.com

ISBN 9788899854713

Printed and bound in the European Union,
Novembre 2017
August 2018 (re-print)

All rights reserved
© of LISt Lab edition;
© of the author's texts;
© of the author's images;

Prohibited total or partial reproduction of this book by any means, without permission of the author and Publisher.

Promotion and distribution in Italy
Messaggerie Libri, Spa,
Milano, (Tel. 800.804.900)
assistenza.ordini@meli.it;

International promotion and distribution
ACC Book Distribution Ltd
Woodbridge, Suffolk,
IP12 4SD, UK
sales@antique-acc.com

he Scientific Committee of the issues List
Eve Blau (Harvard GSD), Maurizio Carta (University of Palermo), Eva Castro (Architectural Association London) Alberto Clementi (University of Chieti), Alberto Cecchetto (University of Venezia), Stefano De Martino (University of Innsbruck), Corrado Diamantini (University of Trento), Antonio De Rossi (University of Torino), Franco Farinelli (University of Bologna), Carlo Gasparrini (University of Napoli), Manuel Gausa (University of Genova), Giovanni Maciocco (University of Sassari/Alghero), Antonio Paris (University of Roma), Mosè Ricci (University of Trento), Roger Riewe (University of Graz), Pino Scaglione (University of Trento), Claudia Battaino (University of Trento), Luca Zecchin (University of Trento).

LISt Lab is an editorial workshop, based in Europe, that works on contemporary issues. LISt Lab not only publishes, but also researches, proposes, promotes, produces, creates networks.

LISt Lab is a green company committed to respect the environment. Paper, ink, glues and all processings come from short supply chains and aim at limiting pollution. The print run of books and magazines is based on consumption patterns, thus preventing waste of paper and surpluses. LISt Lab aims at the responsibility of the authors and markets, towards the knowledge of a new publishing culture based on resource management.